FIRST MATH
PATTERNS

By
Joanna Brundle

KidHaven
PUBLISHING

Published in 2018 by
KidHaven Publishing, an Imprint of Greenhaven Publishing, LLC
353 3rd Avenue
Suite 255
New York, NY 10010

Designer: Danielle Jones
Editor: Joanna Brundle

Cataloging-in-Publication Data

Names: Brundle, Joanna.
Title: Patterns / Joanna Brundle.
Description: New York : KidHaven Publishing, 2018. | Series: First math | Includes index.
Identifiers: ISBN 9781534522084 (pbk.) | ISBN 9781534521926 (library bound) | ISBN 9781534521841 (6 pack) | ISBN 9781534521889 (ebook)
Subjects: LCSH: Pattern perception–Juvenile literature. | Geometry–Juvenile literature. | Mathematics–Juvenile literature.
Classification: LCC BF294.B78 2018 | DDC 516.15–dc23

Printed in the United States of America

CPSIA compliance information: Batch #BS17KL: For further information contact Greenhaven Publishing LLC, New York, New York at 1-844-317-7404.

Please visit our website, www.greenhavenpublishing.com. For a free color catalog of all our
high-quality books, call toll free 1-844-317-7404 or fax 1-844-317-7405.

PHOTO CREDITS

Abbreviations: l-left, r-right, b-bottom,
t-top, c-center, m-middle.

Front cover – Gladskikh Tatiana, ml – suns07butterfly, mr – taviphoto. 3 – 1000 Words. 5 – Designstock. 6 – Chatchawal Kittirojana. 7 – CHAINFOTO24. 8 – Photographee.eu. 9 – Augustcindy. 10 – mady70. 11 – Lana K. 12 – melnikof. 13 – chrisdorney. 14 – pkproject. 15 – virtualimage. 16 – Billion Photos. 17 – Lighthunter. 18 – chiqui. 19 – Africa Studio. 20 – Avella. 21 – Feng Yu. 22 – Ruth Black. 23 – HeinzTeh. 24bl – anetta, bm – Zurijeta, br – Erika Cross.

Images are courtesy of Shutterstock.com, with thanks to Getty Images, Thinkstock Photo, and iStockphoto.

CONTENTS

PATTERNS ARE EVERYWHERE

Supermarket carts in a row make a pattern.

You can see patterns wherever you go.
Patterns are everywhere.

Can you see a pattern on these ice cream cones? ⑤

IN THE GARDEN

 The petals and seeds on this sunflower make a pattern.

A butterfly has the same pattern on both its wings.

There are patterns in this bathroom.
Can you see them on the floor?

This pillow has a zigzag pattern.

TIME

Which season is this?

Our seasons follow a pattern. It goes spring, summer, fall, and winter.

Your day follows a pattern. You get up in the morning and go to sleep at night.

SHAPES

Look for patterns on this quilt.

Shapes can join together to make patterns.

A pattern of squares can make a rectangle.

SPIRALS

snail shells

Snails have a spiral shape on their shells.

This staircase makes a spiral pattern.
Trace the pattern with your finger.

STRIPES

Stripes can make a pattern, too.
Look at these deck chairs.

What colors can you see on these striped socks?

PATTERNS IN NATURE

 There are circle patterns on this tree stump.

Look at this honeycomb and the two busy bees.
Can you see any patterns?

OUT AND ABOUT

20 See if you can spot any patterns on these buildings.

Look out for patterns on the road, such as this crosswalk.

SPOT THE PATTERNS

What patterns can you see?

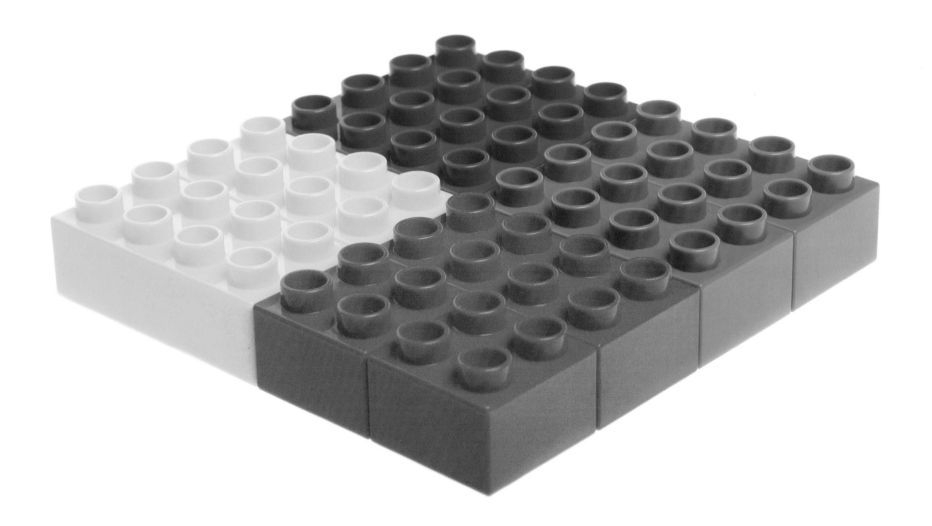

Is there a pattern on these blocks?

FUN WITH PATTERNS

Shout out this pattern of numbers: one, three, five, one, three, five!

1 3 5

Move in this pattern: hop, jump, clap, hop, jump, clap!

Try making some patterns of your own!